SANDRA ROGERS

LESSONS
from the LIGHT

*Insights from a
Journey to the Other Side*

WARNER BOOKS

A Time Warner Company

WARNER BOOKS EDITION

Copyright © 1995 by Sandra Rogers
Foreword © 1995 by Betty J. Eadie
All rights reserved.

Published by arrangement with R. Bemis Publishing, Ltd., Atlanta, GA.

Book design by H. Roberts Design
Cover design by Diane Luger
Cover illustration by Jean-Francois Podevin

Warner Books, Inc.
1271 Avenue of the Americas
New York, NY 10020

 A Time Warner Company

Printed in the United States of America

First Printing: May, 1995

10 9 8 7 6 5 4 3 2 1

These are words from the light . . .

ON ANGELS
- Intuition is your angel's voice.
- Listen to your intuition. If something doesn't seem right, don't do, say, or continue to think it.

ON KINDNESS
- Kindness is a selfless act of love.
- A smile can be a light that ends the spirit of sadness.

ON ANGER AND HAPPINESS
- When we hate others, we hate ourselves.
- When we see someone full of hatred or anger, treat them with love so that you can be an example they may later reflect.

ON DEATH
- Our earthly bodies are mortal, but our spiritual bodies are immortal.
- There are no secrets in the afterlife.

ON SOCIETY
- If everyone knew his or her true nature, there would be peace on earth.
- Just because "everyone does it," doesn't mean that it's right.

This book is dedicated:
To the Light of Love, who understands all and loves unconditionally.

To the volunteers of the world who through their selfless service best reflects the Light of Love.

To my husband, Jack, my son, Blake, and my daughter, Brittany; the family the Light of Love promised me if I'd return to my physical body. They have brought into my life the love and happiness that eluded me in my former life.

They remind me daily that I made the right choice to return to learn their lessons of love.

To Raymond Moody, my friend for eternity, my mentor, and a person the Light told me I'd do something significant with. He is a gentle spirit who is truly an all-weather friend who's given his love freely in darkness and in light. He is a gift to humanity, sent to uncover the Light.

To my mother, Elizabeth Blake, who helped me through the darkest of times, along with my sister, Kaye, and my friends: Barbara, Louise, Pat, David, Allen, Buddy, Pam, Royal, and, of course, Raymond; they never wavered in their love and support of me.

And finally, to Dr. Frank Pratt, Dr. Bob Solenburger, Dr. George Brahn, Dr. Bill Tate, and all the medical staff of the University Hospital, who allowed the Light to work through them as they worked toward my recovery. Also the friends, family members, and co-workers who have not been mentioned thus far, who supported me with visits, prayers, and other acts of love during my recovery.

Thank you.

Acknowledgments

My immense love and appreciation to my husband, Jack, who has given me unwavering love and support during fifteen years of marriage. He has taught me that trust and romantic love can coexist when others before him created ripples of distrust in my life. Jack has given me steadfast love and encouragement throughout the writing of this book, did much of the initial typing, taught me how to use our computer, and assumed the duties of editor prior to submission of the final manuscript. He, along with our children, Blake and Brittany, allowed me to devote a great deal of my time and attention, usually reserved for them, to finishing the manuscript.

I love each of you so very much.

Thank you for making my life complete.

I owe an enormous debt to Royce Bemis for his faith in me. He is not just a publisher, but a true friend. He has learned from his son, David, a teacher in disguise, to share the Light and love with his friends, family, and those who touch his life.

I'm also indebted to Raymond and Cheryl Moody for the love and assurance they give me.

Cheryl, thank you so much for being the answer to my constant prayers for someone to love Raymond and bring him happiness.

Raymond, your gift of love and friendship, which has lasted half of my present life, means more to me than you will ever know. You have been an inspiration and mentor. You, along with Jack, gave me the courage to start writing, and to share with others the experience I shared with you in 1976.

I appreciate your letting me use your findings in this book and I love you, and cherish your support and encouragement.

My mother, Elizabeth Blake, helped me by traveling numerous times from Georgia to Illinois to take care of my children so I could write, make the necessary trips to complete the book, and attend speaking engagements and conferences. I appreciate it and love you more than you will ever know.

My nephew, Marcus McGuire, helped by traveling with my mother and keeping her company. Thanks, Marcus.

My sister and niece, Kaye and Tiffany McGuire, did without them while they were helping me. I appreciate your sacrifice. I love you all.

Others I owe a debt of thanks to are:

Dr. George Ritchie for having the moral courage to tell his story before the "near-death experience" was an accepted phenomenon. He paved the way for other experiencers to share their stories without fear of being labeled "crazy." I appreciate your contribution to this book.

Betty Eadie has used her experience to help so many "see the Light." I thank her for that, and am truly grateful for her contribution to this book.

P.M.H. Atwater continues to do extensive research on NDEs. I sincerely appreciate her allowing me to use her findings in this book.

Peter and Stowe Shockey for their friendship, encouragement, and hospitality.

Valerie Chandler for her friendship and being a constant sounding board.

Anne Hamilton, my editor, for her incredible sense of timing and expertise.

Lonette Brawner for answering phone calls, referring phone calls, and returning phone calls while staying totally unruffled.

The spiritual guidance and inspiration of Dr. Raymond Guterman, Rev. John Grob, Rev. Sylvester Weatherall, and the late Dr. Samuel Heslip.

Two ladies from my childhood who've gone to the Light and who taught me important spiritual lessons: Moma Lola and Lula.

The Light of Love, who is called by many names but is the same for all eternity; and my guardian angels, who help and guide me throughout my daily life.

Contents

Foreword

I first met Sandi Rogers in Houston, Texas, in June, 1994. We were both on the general assembly panel for the first meeting of the International Congress of Enlightenment. The purpose of the assembly was to bring together spiritual thinkers and seekers from around the world, and share spiritual knowledge which would provide enlightenment to guide humanity into the 21st century. During the conference, I had the pleasure of sitting next to Sandi. She told me she was writing a book about the lessons she had learned from her near-death experience. At some point during the conference, she asked me if I would consider writing the foreword. Although I knew Sandi was sincere in her desire to help others, I told her that I would have to read the manuscript before making a commitment. My concern was that perhaps her approach in presenting her insights may spiritually offend some people. But after reading it, I knew LESSONS FROM THE LIGHT could be of tremendous inspiration to everyone.

Sandi's book begins with an introduction, which briefly tells her remarkable life story. It contains a powerful message, because it shows us just how loving God is. Although Sandi's difficult life pushed her down to the depths of despair, where she saw suicide as her only solution, God didn't foresake her, but embraced and uplifted her. He showed Sandi her true spiritual self and let her know just how valuable she was to Him.

I believe the lessons we take from the near-death experience and apply to our daily lives are the most important things we can extract from the experience. Sandi has formatted her message in such a way that the reader can turn to a specific topic, such as angels, love, or wisdom, and find a list of lessons providing insights into that particular aspect of one's spiritual growth. Each section ends with a reflected lesson, in which Sandi further develops the topic by drawing on the experiences and spiritual insights of others who have died and returned.

As you read this book, I would ask that you do so with an open and objective mind, realizing that many of the concepts may be new to you. The intent of this book, I believe, is to cause us to recognize our oneness with God in our spirituality, as opposed to the differences we tend to see in a nonspiritual world, such as different races, religions, cultures and genders.

My sincere hope is that as you read you will think deeply and meditate on these lessons and apply them as you go about your daily life, remembering that the goal for humans is simply that we be a little better today than we were yesterday. As we approach the 21st century, the path we take will decide the destiny of mankind. We can decide to love our neighbors in spite of our differences, by listening, learning, and respecting their ideas. We can learn and understand that God has a purpose for creating our differences, and we must respect each difference as God's creation, perfect for the purpose it serves.

The experiences that Sandi and I, and many others, have shared has forever changed our lives. It stays with us every minute of every day. We want to share it with everyone who touches our lives. But our time on Earth is limited, making it impossible to reach everyone personally. So we have discovered the best way to share our message is through the printed word.

As I see it, the insights given to those who have experienced death and come back and shared them serve the same purpose as talking to a friend or travel agent before going to a foreign country for the first time. There is no way you can learn all you would like to know about the country before visiting, but at least you can prepare yourself for what to expect. Likewise, people who have the near-death experience can't explain everything about the after-life, but they have some information that can make the lives of others who haven't had the experience more tranquil, meaningful and hopeful. If the experiences do nothing else, they let us know our lives are important and meaningful. God wants us to live life abundantly, with love in our hearts for everyone. God wants us to realize that we are called to service; because when we give, we are getting as well. It is our spiritual nature to feel joy when we alleviate suffering and help others. Our spiritual self understands our connection to one another, and thus realizes that by helping others we are actually helping ourselves. God has told us since the beginning of the ages, through prophets and many sacred writings, that we should love one another as ourselves; because God knows what will bring us joy, and God's greatest desire is for our happiness.

Sandi shared with me during our time together in Houston, that before she ever considered writing a book, she had a dream in which she awoke after hearing a voice tell her that a book of lessons, or insights, gained by people who have returned from death would be beneficial to others. She immediately called a friend of hers who is a publisher, and told him about her dream. He told her to write it and send the manuscript to him. The result is LESSONS FROM THE LIGHT. I hope you will let these lessons transform your life by letting the Love of the Light into your life forever. "And above all else—love one another."

Betty J. Eadie

Author's Note

In 1976 I attempted suicide by shooting myself in the chest. Before the ambulance arrived I had what is now commonly referred to as a near-death experience (NDE).

I came into the presence of a brilliant Light who gave me access to unlimited knowledge as long as I remained in the Light. I was told I could remain with the Light, provided I return later to the physical world and experience all that brought me to the point of suicide, along with living the remainder of my life.

I chose the alternative, which was to return to my present physical body to continue the lessons of my current life. I was allowed to take only as much knowledge as I needed to sustain me, and was told I would be given insights along the way as I continued my life. As a result of this experience I have felt compelled to write these insights and to search for the "common thread" that unites the religions of the world. In *Lessons From the Light* I have compiled some of these insights with some of the common insights of others who have had a near-death experience.

Introduction

On the morning of April 30, 1976, following an unsuccessful suicide attempt by drug overdose the previous night, I placed a .38 caliber pistol to my chest, aimed it at my heart and pulled the trigger.

Before the ambulance arrived I had what is now commonly called a near death experience. I came into the presence of a brilliant, wonderfully warm and loving Light. While I was in the presence of this Light I was shown a review of my life and all the events that brought me to that point.

I was fascinated as I watched my life unfold,

that I was aware not only of my own emotions, but also the feelings of those around me as well as those whose lives we touched. I experienced their pain or pleasure and understood what motivated their actions toward others and me.

I watched, as a young child, one of my mother and father's fellow workers attempt to rape my mother, and saw my parents argue because of my father's drinking and squandering what little money we had. I felt his anger and her pain as he occasionally hit her, and watched him point a gun at her and threaten to kill us and himself when she told him she wanted a divorce. I saw the events in his past that motivated his insecurity that caused this behavior. I relived guilt I had at age 4 when my baby sister caught the red measles from me and it developed into meningitis.

During my second grade year my father left us to go to Hollywood to be discovered as a songwriter. I felt the crushing hurt caused by his departure, and again when he returned broken and penniless, finally resulting in my parents' divorce. I saw my sister and me in the middle of the floor as my parents called us from opposite sides of the room to see whom we wanted to go to. I felt like I was dying because I wanted to be with both of them, so I just sat in the middle of the floor and cried. I felt my mother's pain and humiliation from being asked to leave the church because she was a divorced woman, struggling to feed and clothe us, having no money for birthdays or Christmas, and fending off the social worker who was constantly trying to take us away.

I experienced the summer before my fifth grade year when my mother remarried a medically retired veteran. He joined the Army and fought in the jungles with Merrill's Marauders during World War II. When he returned from the war traumatized by its horrors, he was diagnosed as mentally disabled, and had become addicted to the prescription drugs he was given to keep him from having nightmares. I watched and relived the fear and shame of his physical attacks on my mother and his sexual abuse of me. I understood immediately as I relived my torment that his actions were caused by his drug addiction and early exposure during the war to situations where such behavior was condoned. I knew his remorse for what he did was sincere, and I felt his shame and guilt when I tried to commit suicide at the age of thirteen and I was ordered by the court to go live with an aunt and uncle for a while.

My life continued to play on before me and as I watched I relived my young adulthood; I saw the boy I dated throughout high school and re-experienced bittersweet pregnancy and miscarriage in the tenth grade. I was warmed by the happiness of our engagement and saw myself working at a medical lab from four until eight each morning and again in the afternoon following school to save money for our marriage. I felt my anger at being forced to quit my job after being raped by a married co-worker and my humiliation when no one believed me but the rapist's wife. I was devastated by how casually the whole incident was dismissed, and I was left feeling used and utterly worthless.

Later, I saw myself working at a grocery store saving for my wedding until my fiancé hit me during an argument and I broke off the engagement. I felt my anger and pain as he told me that since we had sex no other man would ever love me because I was no longer a virgin. I saw that this incident, coupled with my rape and grandmother's suicide, seemed to confirm my sense of degraded self-worth as a person and as a young woman.

I knew my thrill and elation as I graduated from high school with honors, receiving an award from the office of one of the state senators, only to be slammed back into feelings of despair and rejection when I came home after my stepfather's curfew one night and he refused to let me stay at home any longer.

I felt the horrible fear of moving into the only place I could afford—a run-down apartment in a rough part of town, and getting a job as a cocktail waitress in a nightclub so I could pay my bills. I observed myself letting one of the girls I worked with move into my tiny apartment and relived my being beaten and raped after work one night, and later threatened at gun point by a local bar owner who tried to force me to sleep with him and work as a stripper and prostitute. The final humiliation, before I quit after three months, was having my clothes stolen by the young woman who lived with me.

The feelings of my mother's concern and anxiety flooded over me as I watched her help me move to another apartment, and later back home. Shortly afterward I met and married a college student, became pregnant, miscarried, and got divorced all in rapid succession.

As my life review continued, I encountered again all of the pain and hopelessness of my next several years; a series of bad relationships, pregnancies, miscarriages, broken marriages and suicide attempts. I saw myself as a young woman of twenty-five, married and divorced three times and hospitalized for drug overdoses six times. I felt how I hated my existence and could not understand how a loving God could allow these things to happen.

I was aware as I relived each of these terribly painful events in my life that the Light, which was with me as I watched, felt all of my pain and sorrow and never judged me, but instead understood and loved me.

The love I felt from the Light was overwhelming and I never wanted to leave it. While I was in Its presence I had unlimited knowledge about anything I wanted to know. I was given the choice of remaining with the Light, provided I return later to the physical world and experience all that brought me to the point of shooting myself, or I could return now and pick up my life where it was. I was told that I would eventually have the family and love I so desperately yearned for. I was also told that I could only take back the knowledge I needed to sustain myself, although I would be given insights to help others and me along the way as I continued my life journey.

LESSONS FROM THE LIGHT is my attempt to provide some of the understanding gained through other's and my near-death experiences, as well as insights I have received along the way.

From Experience

"The real study in religion is first-hand experience of God."

The Upanishads:
translated by Swami Prabhavananda
and Frederick Manchester

On Angels

- Angels are God's messengers sent to bring you wisdom.
- Intuition is your angel's voice.
- You are never truly alone. Your angel(s) are always with you.
- Listen to your intuition. If something doesn't seem right, don't do, say, or continue to think it.
- Intuition should be used as your inner guide.
- Angels only need to be asked to intervene in your life.
- Listen to that small, still voice within your

thoughts. It is the voice of your connection with God.

- The gods of one faith are the angels, saints, or other supernatural beings of other faiths.

Reflected Lesson
On Angels

Angels only need to be asked to intervene in your life.

In her best-selling book, *Embraced By The Light,* Betty J. Eadie states that during her near-death experience in 1973, she saw angels rushing to answer prayers. They were filled with much love and joy by their work. These prayers appeared to be beacons of light, illumination of small penlights, and sparks shooting up from the earth.

I was "distinctly told that all prayers of desire are heard and answered," she continues.

"I understood that once our prayers of desire have been released, we need to let go of them and trust in the power of God to answer them. He knows our needs at all times and is simply waiting for an invitation to help us. He has all power to answer prayers, but he is bound by his own law and by our wills. We must invite his will to become our own. We must trust him. Once we have asked with sincere desire, doubting nothing, we will receive."[1]

Betty Eadie's description best depicts the manner in which the light beings, which we call angels, answer prayers. I've heard similar accounts and I was also shown angels (beings of light) engaged in similar actions when in the presence of the Light.

On Anger and Hate

- Anger is love's energy misused.
- When we hate others, we hate ourselves.
- An act of hostility, like a ripple on a pond, radiates out from the giver until eternity.
- Holding a grudge produces negative energy. It not only hurts the one you hold the grudge against, it also hurts you and others.
- As long as you are a child of rage, you will not find the power to know your potential as a child of God.
- When you feel tempted by the emotion of anger—retreat.
- Anger is not the opposite of Love. Indiffer-

ence is. Anger is an expression of our free will, often manifested as a result of feeling controlled and feeling the need to assert our willpower over others.

- In focusing on sex, do so in Love, never in anger. Sex is a gift from God to be given as an expression of Love. Some choose to use sex selfishly, in anger as a weapon, believing it is giving them power and control.
- When you see someone full of hatred or anger, treat them with love so that you can be an example they may later reflect.
- Bigotry is self-hate.
- Vengeance brings only trouble.
- When you teach fear, you create hatred and anger.

Reflected Lesson On
Anger and Hate

When you see someone full of hatred or anger, treat them with love, so that you can be an example they may later reflect.

8

I was shown during my near-death experience that when someone holds a grudge, or is full of hatred and anger, these feelings obscure the positive energy of God's love and light. The anger causes feelings of separateness from the Source of love and light. When a person full of hatred is treated with love, that person is given an opportunity to remember this Source, which helps one put aside the hatred so Light and love may be reflected through that person.

In *Embraced By the Light*, Betty Eadie tells how she was shown the effects of this negative energy.

"When the light is glowing, our core is filled with light and love; it is this energy that gives the body life and power. I saw also that the light could be diminished and the spirit weakened through negative experience—through lack of love, through violence, sexual abuse, or other damaging experiences. By weakening the spirit, these experiences also weaken the body. The body may not get sick, but it is more susceptible then, until the spirit is recharged. We can recharge our own spirits through serving others, having faith in God, and simply opening ourselves to positive energy through positive thoughts. We control it. The source of energy is God and is always there, but we must tune him in."[2]

On Asking, Giving, and Receiving

- The greatest desire of your heart, when granted, can become a burden.
- The greatest burden of your heart can become a blessing.
- Find the blessing in every problem.
- Smile at someone who seems unhappy.
- Give what is needed, when it is needed, without regard to getting in return. Your reward will be greater than you can imagine.
- You are loved so much that if you make a mistake (sin) and ask for God's help and forgiveness, your mistake will be turned into a blessing.

- Love entails giving.
- The only wealth worth having is wealth earned while helping others. Wealth obtained from hurting others is worth nothing.
- Let praises drown out complaints.
- Learn the lesson God gives us in the glorious butterfly. See the physical body as a cocoon that helps in the development of our true self.
- Sharing manifests into abundance.
- Desire is the first stage of receiving abundance.
- In your desire to receive abundance, include your desire to share your abundance with others.
- Desire without action leads to nothing.
- Focus on what you can give, not on what you will get.
- Always give more than required or expected.
- Forgiveness is the capacity to give love in the most difficult circumstances.
- Giving is the most crucial factor in the ability to forgive. You must give love in order to forgive.
- Forgiveness shows God's love in action. It is

as close as we get to God's nature in this physical world.

- Prayer is talking to God. Meditation is listening to God.
- Cries, wishes, hopes, desires, and thoughts are all forms of prayer.
- God wants us to have abundance. You will have physical abundance if what you are doing is spiritually fulfilling.

Reflected Lesson on
Asking, Giving, and Receiving

Forgiveness shows God's love in action. It is as close as we get to God's nature in this physical world.

When I was in the Light during my near-death experience, seeing my life, and the effects of my thoughts and actions on others, I felt total forgiveness and love from the Light. The Light knew the motivation behind my thoughts and actions, as well as the thoughts and actions of others who touched my life. Nothing was hidden. The result was total understanding and total forgiveness.

In *Embraced By The Light*, Betty Eadie tells how she was shown how we are to love one another. She states, "I was shown that love is supreme. I saw that truly without love we are nothing. We are here to help each other, to care for each other, to understand, forgive, and serve one another."[3]

On Bodies

- Our earthly bodies mask the abilities of our spiritual bodies.
- Our spiritual body, when separated from our physical body, can be several places at once.
- It's easier to get from person to person than from person to place when separated from our physical body because we are all spiritually connected.
- Communication in the spiritual body is telepathic. Your thoughts are answered in thought as rapidly as your mind can send and receive them.
- Growing old is a natural weaning process for

transition from the physical body to the spiritual body.

- Ancestry of the body is far less important than the ancestry of the spirit.

- Pain is caused by too much focus on the physical attributes of the physical body.

- While in the physical body, our lives are lived from the inside to the outside.

- When your mind is in a state of negativity, your body will follow.

- If you fail to forgive, your body will hold that negative energy within and slowly destroy itself.

- Jesus was born through the physical ancestry of a woman whose lineage was equally representative of the three major races. Therefore, Jesus, born a Jewish male, was representative of the entire human race in his physical form.

- The energy within our physical body is the essence of perfection and only needs to be uncovered to shine.

- From the point of view of our conscious mind, life's not fair, but our spiritual being knows there's a purpose to our dilemmas: to experience in order to gain knowledge.

- Our soul is a part of the body of God; therefore, it is immortal and eternal.

- Females are generally more intuitive, therefore they are usually more in touch with the Light energy than males.

- Exercise your Spirit through meditation.

- Exercise your brain through thought.

- Disease in the physical body is caused when there is a disturbance between the spiritual body and the physical body. Most often the disturbance is due to some form of excess, or deprivation.

- Just as the smallest atom of your physical body is part of you, you are part of God.

- The physical body is a temporary shelter for the spiritual body.

- The spirit is infinite, and everlasting.

- When the physical and spiritual bodies are at battle, growth is impeded.

- Matter is mass thought.

- When you are scared, remember you are a spirit, and sacred.

- Your true self is infinite, spaceless, endless, timeless, ageless, indestructible, and tireless.

- A smile helps the soul shine through the internal to the external.
- The cells of your physical body are made of light.
- Thought can bring loved ones near in spirit even though they are physically far away.
- You are not a physical body made of flesh and bones, but a part of God who is Light, Love, and infinite.
- Hardships are necessary for the growth of our spiritual bodies.

Reflected Lesson
On Bodies

Disease in the physical body is caused when there is a disturbance between the spiritual body and the physical body. Most often the disturbance is due to some form of excess, or deprivation.

I was shown during my life that our free will was the reason for the suffering and sorrow in the world.

If we didn't exercise our free will to go against God's will, we would have peace and harmony on earth. We decide to dwell on negative thoughts, thus creating pain, suffering, and sorrow. We decide not to have balance in our lives; therefore disease exists. We decide to overeat, to create images of desirability that seduce people to undereat, to get drunk, and to become addicted to drugs. When we act and think in this manner, we are creating. What we are creating is disharmony, which results in disease, pain, sorrow, and suffering.

Betty Eadie explained in *Embraced By The Light* that she was shown that "There is a cause and effect relationship to sin. We create many of our own punishments through the actions we commit. If we pollute the environment, for example, this is a 'sin' against the earth, and we reap the natural consequences of breaking the laws of life. We may be weakened physically or die because of our actions. There are also sins against the flesh such as over-eating or under-eating, lack of exercise, drug abuse (which includes using any substances not in harmony with the organization of our bodies), and other physically debilitating actions. No one of these 'sins' of the flesh is greater than another. We are responsible for our bodies."[4]

On Children

- The spirits that God sends to be our children will be the same regardless of the manner they become our children.
- Those born with mental or physical afflictions are spiritually higher beings born to help others evolve spiritually.
- Childhood is necessary so the spiritual body can adjust to the limits of the physical body.
- Most younger children have memories of their life before their birth, but those memories are dismissed as imagination by parents and others.
- The physical body the spirit enters is chosen

prior to birth. When the life of a physical body is terminated prior to birth, the advancement of the spirit is interrupted.

- Spirits choose to be born to parents who will help with their spiritual advancement as well as the spiritual advancement of the parents.

- Spirits who choose lifetimes which end in childhood deaths often feel the need to comfort the parents with after-death visits.

Reflected Lesson
On Children

Spirits who choose lifetimes which end in childhood deaths often feel the need to comfort the parents with after-death visits.

While in the Light I was given an opportunity to receive complete knowledge, but later focused on areas of concern to me.

One area I had difficulty understanding was why children had to die. I was shown that the children had planned their own spiritual journey, a spiritual journey best for their spiritual growth and the growth of their parents. At their deaths the children know of their parents' suffering, and realize their parents do not understand their death. To comfort their parents, they feel the need to visit them after death to reassure them that they are happy in the afterlife.

Dr. Raymond Moody, in his book *Reunions: Visionary Encounters with Departed Loved Ones,* states "Clinical experience reveals that apparitions of the deceased are common among other bereaved groups too—children, parents, siblings, and friends of the deceased. For instance, as many as 75 percent of parents who lose a child will have some kind of apparition of the child within a year of the loss. This experience is a relief for most of the parents and will greatly reduce their grief."[5]

On Death

- Our earthly bodies are mortal, but our spiritual bodies are immortal.
- When you die, everything you have said, thought, or done will be known by all.
- There are no secrets in the afterlife.
- Spirits with like thoughts are drawn to each other in the afterlife.
- If an addiction isn't conquered before your physical death, it could keep your spirit earthbound.
- After life, you take with you what you are, not what you own.

- Moderation during physical life is the key to a successful transition to the spirit world.

- Dying is merely a transition to another world.

- Death is only a change from one state of existence to another.

- There are many domains of learning, and Earth is only one.

- Grief for a lost loved one is like the pain felt by mothers who experience "the empty-nest syndrome." It is only a temporary loss, because they have only gone to their next stage of life.

- We can help a deceased loved one's spiritual transition through prayer. Prayer helps because of our connection of love with that person.

- In our physical life we continually search for answers to the "why" of life. When we die we will know the "why."

- We have nothing to fear from death. Death isn't painful; it's a very peaceful, tranquil transition. What causes most of us to fear death are the conditions which bring us to death.

- We do not need to fear life after death.

- Spirits with evil thoughts avoid the Light at death because they are too ashamed to have their life revealed.

- Death is a transition from the physical life to another existence where there is no pain and suffering, unless we choose to remain away from the Light.

- Going to the Light after death, all resentfulness, vindictiveness, and conflicts vanish as full understanding of motivations is revealed in the life review.

- Death does not exist for our spirit; our physical ending is just another beginning.

- If you understand the transition we call death, you will no longer have fear. You may fear the events surrounding death, but not death itself.

- Selfishness, not selflessness, holds a suffering loved one in the physical body when it's time for them to go to the Light.

- Death, as the end of life, is an illusion.

- Physical death is a new spiritual beginning.

Reflected Lesson
On Death

If an addiction isn't conquered before your physical death, it could keep your spirit earthbound.

I learned during my near-death experience that there were spiritual bodies that chose not to go to the Light. Free will still exists beyond the physical body. Often the reason they didn't go to the Light is they'd developed an addiction while in the physical body. They became so focused on the addiction that they do not desire to go to the Light. Instead they stay earthbound in their spiritual bodies, trying endlessly to obtain that to which they are addicted. Dr. George Ritchie, author of *Return From Tomorrow* and *My Life After Dying: Becoming Alive to Universal Love,* was shown several examples of this during his NDE in 1943.

In *Return From Tomorrow,* Dr. Ritchie states, "I saw a group of assembly-line workers gathered around a coffee canteen. One of the women asked another for a cigarette, begged her in fact, as though she wanted it more than anything in the world. But the other one, chatting with her friends, ignored her. She took a pack of cigarettes from her coveralls, and without offering it to the woman who reached for it so eagerly, took one out and lit it. Fast as a striking snake the woman who had been refused snatched at the lighted cigarette in the other one's mouth. Again she grabbed at it. And again . . . With a little chill of recognition I saw she was unable to grip it." Dr. Ritchie continues to explain that this woman and others were earthbound spiritual bodies, and were substance-less without the aureole of light that surrounded the physical bodies of those still alive.[6]

On Free Will

- God gives us opportunities for growth experiences throughout life; using them is our choice.
- The thoughts you feed your subconscious affect your spiritual body the way the food you eat affects your physical body.
- Do what you love to do (what your spirit leads you to do) and you will do it well.
- There is accountability for everything you do or think, even what you *think* you got away with.
- Hell is a state of being which we are capable

of creating and spending the rest of eternity in until we choose to return to God.

- The self has free will to create pain from sin in the physical world and carry it to the spiritual world, thus creating hell.

- It is your right to be free in what you think, say, and do as long as you realize it's your right only as long as it doesn't infringe on the rights of others.

- The way we think about everythingdetermines the effect it has on us. This defines our beliefs.

- Life is a series of causes and effects. Even what we call fate, luck, or destiny has a cause which begins in our thoughts.

- The same energy used to cause fear can be used to end that fear, and create a desired effect.

- If you want a pleasant life, fill your mind with pleasant thoughts.

- The one thing a person can do to make a difference in the way a life is going is to change the way one thinks.

- There are limitations to the human will. There are no limitations to the spiritual will.

- Belief is the beginning of an action. If you want the action of a miracle to happen, you must believe.
- Creation is born of thought. Construction is born of thought and action.
- Thoughts are acts. When the thought is coveting, the coveted object will eventually appear, or come to pass. This is why we are commanded not to covet that which is not ours, or not good.
- Thoughts should be free flowing. A flexible tree bends with the wind; a rigid tree breaks.
- Thoughts that are consistent manifest themselves into our actions.
- We should focus our thoughts on how we can help, rather than what we can help.
- We should exercise moderation in all that we do. Overindulgence in anything will bring a burden to our life.
- For peace of mind, always allow yourself some quiet time.
- Faith can create miracles.
- Closed minds are not open to abundance. Open minds are ready to receive abundantly.
- Desire is thought impulse.

- Thoughts will become manifest: therefore it is best to feed your mind thoughts of Love rather than thoughts of fear or hate.
- Dreams without action remain dreams.
- Life's greatest mistakes can be traced back to fear.
- Failure occurs when thoughts of indecision, doubt, and dread predominate.
- Thought put to proper use can produce miracles.
- Reality begins with thought.
- You and you alone decide how to perceive and use your life experience.
- Obstacles are opportunities in disguise.
- What you decide for yourself will be.
- Behavior is always the result of the thought that immediately preceded it.
- What you do shows more of who you are than what you say.
- To have abundance, do what you do with love, and love what you do.
- The belief that we are limited is an illusion. We are limited only by our beliefs.
- Anything you can think of with your mind can be produced in the physical world.

- If you spend your time wondering why "they" get to do, get to have, or get to be, instead of pursuing what "you" want to do, want to have, or want to be, you'll never obtain what you want.

- Greed comes from fear of the illusion of limited supply. God created more than enough for all to live abundantly.

- Thoughts, the decisions based on these thoughts, and actions resulting from decisions are based on free will, given by God, and controlled by each individual.

- Anything that is learned by your body, mind, and spirit will be remembered.

- If you make a mistake, don't lament it; turn it into a blessing.

- Desire has to be greater than fear for success to be achieved. Indecision, doubt, and fear are the enemies of success.

- Our mind can create or destroy. Choose peace and harmony instead of conflict and discord.

- Decide to be happy at all times. Decide to find happiness within yourself and eventually you will find it.

- A restless mind finds it difficult to find happiness. When feelings of restlessness invade your peaceful soul, seek God through meditation until your calm spirit is restored.

- God does not punish, He only loves. He has given us free will to grow in knowledge and find happiness. Every thought or action causes a reaction by which we must live with the consequences. As an example, if I choose evil over good I suffer the natural consequences which I may perceive as God punishing me.

Reflected Lesson
On Free Will

The self has free will to create pain from sin in the physical world and carry it, in thought form, to the spiritual world, thus creating hell.

Both physical and spiritual bodies have free will, and in the afterlife, there are those who choose not to go to the Light. Often the reason they choose not to go is the contents of their thoughts. In the afterlife there are no secrets. Communication occurs through thought waves. Spirits who have thoughts they want to hide avoid going into the Light, so they go where they feel most comfortable, with spirits of like thoughts.

Dr. George Ritchie, in his book *My Life After Dying: Becoming Alive to Universal Love,* explains, "There were definite areas of this dimension that I would not want to be caught in, just as there are areas in our own towns and cities that we don't feel safe in. Since hypocrisy is impossible because others know your thoughts the minute you think them, they tend to group with the ones who think the same way they do. In our own plane of existence, earth, we have a saying: 'Birds of a feather flock together.' The main reason that they stick together is because it is too threatening to be with beings with whom you disagree when they know it." He further explains what he was later shown: "What I saw horrified me more than anything I have ever seen in life. Since you could tell what the beings of this place thought, you knew they were filled with hate, deceit, lies, self-righteousness bordering on megalomania, and lewd sexual aggressiveness that were causing them to carry out all kind of abominable acts on each other. This was breaking the heart of the Son of God standing beside me. Even here were angels trying to get them to change their thoughts. Since they could not admit there were beings greater than themselves, they could not see or hear them. There was no fire and brimstone here: no boxed-in canyons, but something a thousand times worse from my point of view. Here was a place totally devoid of love. This was HELL."[7]

This is a place created by free will.

On Kindness

- Show kindness without expecting anything in return and you will be rewarded tenfold.
- Kindness is a selfless act of love. Kindness yields friends.
- A simple act of kindness, like a ripple on a pond, radiates from the giver throughout eternity.
- React to the faults of others as kindly as you do with your own faults.
- If practice makes perfect, why not practice being good?
- Go where you can do good, and you will find you don't have to travel far.

- Practice kindness by acting as if the motive of behavior is known to all.
- When you radiate feelings of sympathy, empathy, and goodwill, you open yourself to receive the fullness of God's love.
- When you treat "enemies" with forgiveness, understanding, friendliness, humility, and love, eventually the time will come when they will open up and no longer reject your offer of kindness.
- See your "enemy" as your equal who is temporarily blinded by misunderstanding.
- A smile can be a light that ends the spirit of sadness.

Reflected Lesson
On Kindness

A simple act of kindness, like a ripple on a pond, radiates from the giver throughout eternity.

During my life review, I saw and experienced everything I did and thought before and during my life, including the effects of my actions on others. This went on to include the people they affected as a result of my thoughts and actions, and so on, like a domino effect. I felt these effects as though I were living each action. As my thoughts and actions merged with the thoughts and actions of others, the effects became less clear and the feelings less distinct.

Dr. Raymond A. Moody, Jr., in his book *The Light Beyond,* describes a composite of this part of the NDE. "In this situation, you also see every action that you have ever done, but you also perceive immediately the effects of every single one of your actions upon the people in your life. So for instance, if I see myself doing an unloving act, then immediately I am in the consciousness of the person I did that act to, so that I feel their sadness, hurt, and regret. On the other hand, if I do a loving act to someone, then I am immediately in their place and I feel the kind and happy feelings. Through all of this, this Being (of Light) is with those people (experiencers), asking them what good they have done with their lives."[8]

In other words, you really do reap what you sow.

On Love and God

- God sends truth through many channels to those who ask.
- Love creates positive energy.
- Indifference is the opposite of love.
- You are a part of God, and God is a part of you.
- Everything is a part of God.
- God works for our best interests.
- When we work with God, we create love.
- Every action of love has a reaction of joy.
- Others judge us by our actions; God judges us by our motivations.

- All you do and think is known to God, and God understands everything.
- The greatest joy is to share love.
- Transformation occurs through the energy of love.
- God (the Light) knows you for who you are.
- We are all one with God, and to hurt even the smallest part of God hurts us all.
- Light is the single source through which all are united.
- Selflessness turns energy into the power of Love.
- When you see the Light everywhere, and see everything in the Light, the Light will never be lost to you, nor will you be lost to the Light.
- The secret to power is to make and keep yourself connected to the Light of Love (God), which is our constant source of energy.
- God loves and forgives you, and expects you to love and forgive others.
- Love, like God, is too immense and profound to ever be fully understood, measured,

or confined within the structure of the physical world's concept of language.

- In human terms, love can best be defined as the willingness to give of one's self for the spiritual knowledge and development of others as well as one's self.
- Love at its best is Love motivated to action.
- Remind people of Love by word—written and spoken.
- In terms of seeing the life force as energy, we have to get back to the right love frequency before we can be unified with God, the ultimate life force.
- All pain we feel or cause is felt by the Light.
- God is spirit, which is the energy that creates all.
- God is the cause. Life is the effect.
- The part of man causing effects is the part of man in the image and of the essence of God.
- To honor God, the effects we cause should be worthy of God.
- In the beginning man thought of himself as separate from God, and lost sight of his oneness with God.
- In order to become one with God, work

must be done to remember or find the truth, which is your true self is a spirit and that spirit is one with God.

- Love requires committing yourself to the spiritual growth of others without the guarantee of love returned.

- Sleep is a time in which our spiritual body connects in a focused manner with God to recharge our energy.

- It's not possible for one who has experienced and remembers the infinite to completely explain it in finite language.

- The Love that shines brightest is that which reflects on others.

- Enjoy the simple beauty of God's artwork; it surrounds you.

- No amount of darkness can blot out light, yet the tiniest amount of light can overcome darkness.

- The only thing that lives forever is Love.

- Praise God for the things you have, and also for what you do not have.

- Love endures forever.

- God's paradise for us is Love. We can create

paradise again if we learn to love one another as ourselves.

- Where Love dwells, God is there.
- Our interrelatedness is the reason and the way that all things work together for good. Everything God makes has a purpose in creating good.
- All the good in creation is a result of Love.
- In the search for truth and understanding, all paths lead to Love.
- Since we are created from God, we work with God, not for God.
- Always want the best for your enemies. The best is Love.
- Miracles happen when you realize that God is your source and you place your trust in God. God is limitless.
- The mind is the builder of the physical world.
- Nothing is secret. Our thoughts are being recorded for all to hear, see, and experience. What you do in secret is known.
- To live in the Light is to let Love be your motivator.

- God is the one energy from which all other energies are manifested.
- God is, Death isn't.[9]
- Life is a road full of lessons teaching Love. When Love is learned, you will forever be home.
- Work is Love demonstrated.
- Through God even the impossible is possible.
- God is infinite Love, laughter, energy, Light, and infinite wisdom.
- God is in all places at all times.
- When you fully understand your true self, nothing can destroy you.
- Love in the physical world is a reflection of Love throughout eternity.
- God is Love, Light, and the energy in all. God is the source of perfect Love and all life.

Reflected Lesson On
Love and God

Since we are created from God, we work with God, not for God.

During my NDE I followed my angel guide into the Light. The angel was absorbed by the Light and so was I. While in the Light I learned that everything in existence was created from the essence of God, the Light. After God created man, the gift of free will was given to each of us, giving us the power of the essence to create. But man has forgotten this ability.

Since man has forgotten that thoughts start this creative process, man has created a world of disharmony rather than a world of peace and harmony. We need to remember we are created from God, so we are co-creating with God. We should honor God with a world that would bring Love and joy to the universe.

Dr. Ritchie asserted this in his book *My Life After Dying: Becoming Alive to Universal Love:* "So God created man (male and female) in His image. Now we are told in most denominations of the Christian religion that no one has seen God, but we have seen the One God was referring to when He said to the One with Him from the beginning, His Son, let us create man in Our Image."

Dr. Ritchie continues, "Everything that I

can think of that God created in man is neutral.
God left it to man to decide how he was going
to use his faculties. But the whole man, as we
have seen in the Christ, uses his attributes to ex-
press love and to accept it. Therefore in all the
departments of his life, he is governed by love
for himself and others. I put it this way because
we really can't see others as lovable until we see
ourselves as lovable."[10]

Since we've been given this ability, we need
to use it to create a world of harmony to honor
God rather than a world of disharmony, which
dishonors God.

On Other Gods

- An addiction is giving your God-given power to a material substance.
- That which controls you in the physical world will control you in the spiritual world.
- Anything you need, or believe you need, controls you.
- Anything you are addicted to controls you. To end the addiction, you must take back the power of controlling your thoughts.
- When you have habits, or addictions, that negatively affect others, you are choosing that substance or behavior over God.
- Beliefs create limits.

- Idolatry means giving some habit, or object, primary focus in your life, rather than enjoying spiritual growth through loving others.
- Pursuits of the physical life bring only temporary happiness.
- Resist the temptation of the earthly matters that keep your thoughts away from God.
- When we become too attached to material things, we tend to forget God.

Reflected Lesson On
Other Gods

Beliefs create limits.

I was shown during my NDE that what we believe creates our reality and can control us. I was also shown that the phrase "other gods" didn't refer to angels, or other names given to "super-natural" beings, altars, or statues; "other gods" means that which we relinquish control of our lives to. Examples of "other gods" would be alcohol, cigarettes, other abused drugs, money, jobs, or anything that can control you, or that you have allowed to create the belief that you can't exist without this "other god." When this happens, it interferes with your spiritual life and the spiritual lives of those you touch. If you allow these beliefs to limit you, you will focus on them and they will hold you captive until you believe you can't leave them behind when you die. Therefore, you'll desire to stay with that which you believe you can't "live without" instead of focusing on the Light, the true God.

Dr. George Ritchie reflects on the effect our beliefs have on us in his book *My Life After Dying*. He explains, "So I hear God asking man where is he in relation to Himself, i.e., is he accepting just the instincts and urges of his physical ego or self, or is he in communion with God through his higher spiritual self, and the Holy Spirit within himself? Man has to believe something before he can act upon it. Our thoughts or beliefs create emotions. Emotions create feeling. Feelings are the things that govern our actions, not our intelligence or truths. If we believe a lie is true, we are going to act and react on or to it. Since we are creative beings, then our beliefs in lies create further lies and further separation from God since God is truth."[11]

On Religion

- The universe is God's Church.
- Religion is a cultural institution.
- The church universal is all the children of God who seek truth, so they can live a life of love.
- A wrathful and threatening god is a god of man's creation.
- The more spiritually evolved one is, the more one sees truth in different religions: one less spiritually evolved sees only difference.
- The problem with institutionalizing God's church through religions is that each religion tries to limit that which is limitless. God cre-

ated differences because there are different ways to serve God, and different lessons we all need to learn.

- Religions are man's attempt to understand and worship God, but in doing so they limit God, who is limitless.

- Any religion, or denomination, that attempts to restrict your association with others not of your particular belief is worshiping their idea of God, not God.

- Truth doesn't bind others.

- Ignorance is so fixed in beliefs, it does not allow the spirit of truth in.

- To be fixed in beliefs is to try to make the infinite finite.

- Our purpose in the physical body has nothing to do with believing in doctrine, or dogma, written by others, but in being and becoming one with God.

- Names and images given to God are not important, nor do they explain God. These names and images are only man's symbols of God.

- There are many religions because man's nature is to adapt truth to his particular circumstances.

- Those who seek to do good are on the quickest path to God.
- If members of the various world religions practiced the lessons taught by the teachers these religions are based on, the world would be a peaceful place.
- There is one God who is worshiped through many different teachings of many different religious faiths.
- God is in all of us. God is male and female, all races, and the reason for all religions.
- There are only two "real" religions on this earth, the religion of love and the religion of fear, and everyone belongs to one, or the other, regardless of what they may claim.[12]

Reflected Lesson
On Religion

If members of the various world religions practiced the lessons taught by the teachers the religions are based on, the world would be a peaceful place.

Throughout the history of man, God has sent truth for us to live by. We have perverted this truth to suit our society, and those in authority have twisted the truth to control those not in power. God sent teachers and prophets to restate the truth, but civilizations formed religions based on religious leaders rather than focusing on the truth they brought, thereby perpetuating the cycle.

Dr. George Ritchie states in his book *My Life After Dying: Becoming Alive to Universal Love:* "Even in this world we say in our courts that ignorance of the law is no excuse. How much more is this true of God's universe and in nature on this planet. It is my belief that a loving God does not send catastrophe upon us: we bring it upon ourselves because we won't listen to Him, to His Son or to the prophets and great leaders of all times that He sent trying to guide us. If you and I are one of the messengers who have been given a chance to meet Him or one of His beings of love and light He has sent to us, and we remain silent when we see the people in our world creating a 'diverse' instead of a universe, then we are guilty of not doing our part.

Yes, it cost Jesus and the prophets their lives when they spoke out against the wrong practices of the organized religion and corrupt governments of their times. It has always been hard to stand for the difficult right against the easy wrong." 13

Finding the truth takes effort on the part of the seeker. Truth requires more than simply going to church and accepting all that church leaders state as truth. Seekers must actively participate by searching for the common truths sent to mankind by God.

Another Reflected Lesson on Religion

Dr. Ritchie remarks in the "Reflected Lesson On Values" that the world can now be traveled in a day, due to our technological advancements (refer to footnote #17). In the future, we will have business and social contacts with people of other cultures more often. It is in the best interests of everyone that we practice the lessons from the Light and be aware that the

Light is present in the sacred writings of all the major world religions. I haven't found a religion in my research where the afterlife is broached in depth where the Light isn't mentioned or referred to. We are all worshiping the one God and we are part of God's family. We must learn to embrace the common aspects of the world religions and respect the differences as those of cultural influence. When we practice this lesson we will finally begin to see peace on Earth.

On Self and Others

- You are much more than you think you are. Others are much more than you think they are.
- What you do affects others in ways you never see. What you don't do affects others in ways you never see.
- We are what we choose to be. We are what we think. God gives us the tools; it's up to us to use them.
- As you forgive, you will be forgiven, and you will live the results you create for others.
- You will eventually know the motivation of others who have touched your life.

- When you criticize others, you are belittling yourself.
- Life provides opportunities to give love by healing the hurts of others.
- Energy not expressed in love can be hurtful to others and to yourself.
- You will be judged as you judge others. Your prosecutor will be yourself.
- Leading a moral life consists of being true to your spiritual self (doing God's will) and treating others as you want to be treated.
- If you make a mistake, admit it rather than blaming others. Casting blame only serves to magnify your mistake in the eyes of others.
- When you meet a person trying to abide by God's will, emulate him or her. When you meet a person not abiding by God's will, do not judge them, but look within your own heart.
- A person's true character shows during times of adversity.
- If you want to find happiness, look for those in pain and help them.
- To conquer envy or covetousness when you

see riches, wealth or physical features you desire, find someone who has less than you.

- Respect others as you wish to be respected. Hurt no one, and if you are hurt, ask God to bless your abuser.

- Be thankful for what is yours while appreciating what others have or have created, without being covetous.

- Being a good neighbor means you are mindful of the rights of others before asserting your own will.

- Don't blame others for the crimes of their ancestors. Their ancestors are your ancestors too.

- Repentance is becoming consciously aware of our sins and their effect on ourselves and others, then making a conscious decision to change and correct them.

- Selfishness delights in receiving for one's self: selflessness delights in giving to others.

- Through selflessness the giver becomes the receiver of the gift of gratitude and goodwill.

- We are all able to go beyond self to tap into our oneness with God.

- The secret to stopping sexual harassment,

slander, etc. is helping others understand that not only do their actions affect others, but will come back to them.

- All you do to others, you do to yourself. If you hurt others, you will be hurt. If you love others, you will be loved.
- You don't lose when you give. You receive.
- What you allow to happen to others also happens to you.
- In reviewing our life, the pain we cause others for personal pleasure is more hurtful than pain we cause others in defending ourselves, defending others, or for a cause we believe is honorable.
- In reviewing our life, the joy we feel from helping others is more pleasurable when the intent is selfless rather than selfish.
- The love and joy we feel during our life review is the same as we've shown to others during our life.
- Anointing a person with oil is a means of conducting energy through a person's physical body. The oil is used much like the conductive jelly put on a patient before a defibrillator is used on them during resuscitation.

- That which you loathe in others is the very aspect you forbid yourself.

- Give others unconditional Love, and you will receive inconceivable joy.

- In considering others, do so based on character proven by words and deeds rather than by categories, such as race, creed, gender, or color.

- Do something nice for someone you don't know without any expectation of gratitude.

- When you are with others who've forgotten their Source and don't reflect Love, pray for their enlightenment rather than allowing their negativity to dim the Light that shines within you.

- Reach out to others with love in your heart.

- Everything one does or thinks affects everything else.

- No life is meaningless.

- In order to forgive, you must understand. When you recognize that you are spiritually connected to others, you will find it's easier to treat others as you would like to be treated.

- Peace begins with cooperation. Cooperation

begins with seeing connection rather than separateness.

- Conflict exists because of decisions made to control the actions of others.

- When you make critical or judgmental remarks about others you know, or know of, the people you make the remarks to wonder what you say about them when they are not listening.

- Be careful when you say that a victim of a crime was "asking to become a victim" because of their actions or inaction. You may find yourself, or someone close to you, in a similar position at some time in order that you might understand the crime was caused by the free will of the criminal, not the victim.

- If you trap someone in a situation, you will also be trapped.

- Be a blessing to others.

- Even those who say they do not believe in God believe in energy and/or a life force; therefore, they do actually believe in God, they just have not figured out a name for "God" yet.

- Uplift those who are brought into your life. Wish for others that which you wish for yourself.

- Think of yourself as a vibration of peaceful Love. Spread happiness to everyone you meet.

- Those who are brought into your life are there to love and help you. Ask for God's help to see the essence of God in everyone you meet.

- In working for the well-being of others, you will be guided to prosperity.

- Let it be your heart's desire that someone who has hurt you will be blessed.

- What you think is where your heart will be.

- As you judge, you will be judged.

- The true self is the thought creator, not the form it created.

- Your secret thoughts are known.

Reflected Lesson On
Self and Others

*Everything one does or thinks affects
everything else.*

While going through my life review during my near-death experience. I felt as if I were both watching and participating. I was in the Light, and the Light was also watching and participating.

I felt how my thoughts and actions affected others, and how their thoughts and actions affected me. The motivations causing these thoughts and actions were also known. My understanding was more distinct the closer I was to the immediate thought or action. As my thoughts and actions connected with thoughts and actions of others, they became increasingly less clear.

In describing her 1977 near-death experience in her book *Coming Back To Life: The After-effects of Near-Death Experience*, P.M.H. Atwater states that her life review wasn't so much a review, but ". . . a total reliving of every thought, word, and deed I had ever done; plus the effects of each thought, word and deed on everyone and anyone who had ever come within my environment or sphere of influence whether I knew them or not (including unknown passersby on the street); plus the effect of each thought, word, and deed on weather, plants, animals, soil, trees, water, and air."[14]

Another Reflected Lesson On Self and Others

Even those who say they do not believe in God believe in energy and/or a lifeforce; therefore, they do actually believe in God, they just have not figured out a name for "God" yet.

I learned during my near-death experience that subconsciously we are all aware of God's existence since we all exist because God exists. When people deny God's existence, it is usually someone else's concept of God they are denying, such as the concept of God as a giant man with a long white beard up in the sky.

During the Soviet Union's war with Afghanistan, the field commander of the Soviet troops, General Slava Borisov, discovered this. General Borisov was in a helicopter that was shot down by rebel fire and crashed. He was a devout atheist upon entering the helicopter, but was a devout believer in God before the helicopter hit the ground. "As my helicopter spun out of control, I cried out to God. And I did it subconsciously, I did it instinctively. And I cried out to Him, 'God save me.' I survived, fortunately, even though I was wounded very severely." Borisov was the only survivor among twelve people in the helicopter when it crashed. This convinced him it was God's intervention that saved him. He continued, "I came to the idea that there is a super power, a super force in the universe—which is God—that can help people in difficult situations when nobody else can help. I turned to this power. . . . I found out how powerful God is and if you pray to Him and have fellowship with Him, He'll help you and He'll never let you down, no matter what kind of circumstances, you are going through."[15]

On Sin and Sorrow

- We have free will to work *against* God. When we work against God, we create turmoil!
- Every action of sin has a reaction of pain.
- The words that are most evil are those intended to hurt someone.
- There is no unforgivable sin.
- Adversity builds character.
- Sin causes suffering. Because we are connected spiritually, when we sin we suffer and cause others to suffer. We are never the only one affected.
- When a sin committed by one person affects

another, the sinner is indebted to that person in proportion to the effect of the sin.

- Sins are committed by word, deed, and thought.
- Our spirit hurts when we do that which we know is wrong.
- Rape is the vilest of crimes because it not only harms the physical body, it also hurts the spiritual body.
- As long as there is sin, disease and suffering will be in the world.
- Man's misuse of free will causes suffering and disease.
- God transforms the results of man's sins into opportunities to learn love.
- It is best to think of sin as the mistake of forgetting our oneness with God.
- The fig leaf symbolizes fear obstructing God's light in you.
- The forbidden fruit symbolizes the spiritual body entering the physical body and starting the spiritual body's desire for things of the physical world.
- All suffering can be ended through forgiveness.

- Sin is a lie. It deceives us into believing we are what we are not. Sin makes us believe we are limited. It makes us believe life is limited, and that we should get all we can while we are able.

- Blaming someone else is like picking at a scab; it keeps the wound from healing.

- Trouble, pain, and/or conflict sometimes happens because we unconsciously are aware it is needed to help another person, or persons, to grow.

- Evil happens because of man's self-centeredness.

- God will never give us more than we can withstand because we always have the ability to leave our physical body when pain gets unbearable.

- Anything can be endured when there is Love.

- Suffering began with free will, but is transformed by Love into good by helping to further develop our spiritual growth.

- The seed to all sin is seeing self as separate from others, creating the illusion that the deeds of self will not cause harm to others.

- Our sins are relived in God's Light during every transition from one life to another; therefore the results of our sins are felt by the Light.
- To live only in the physical world is to burden yourself with pain and suffering.
- Guilt only causes pain. Only action to gain forgiveness can rectify another's feelings about your past behavior.
- Satan and demons are what you make them. Evil exists because we fear and think unkind thoughts.
- Giving help to others to overcome sorrows brings ultimate joy.
- Evil is good misapplied.
- The first sin was selfishness.
- When you try to get even, things get even worse.
- Dishonesty, or lies, breeds discord.
- Evil flourishes where good people choose not to involve themselves in stopping it.
- Adversity increases dependence on God.
- Life in the physical world is a struggle to find true happiness.

- And hardship is easier when we acknowledge God's presence.
- Sins are actions, or inaction, that hurt you and others.
- Victory can lead to hatred if it creates sorrow for the losers or pride for the winners.

Reflected Lesson On
Sin and Sorrow

The seed to all sin is seeing self as separate from others, creating the illusion that the deeds of self will not cause harm to others.

During my NDE, I saw that we are all connected, therefore all our actions and thoughts affect all that exists. I was shown that the reason we should treat others as we would want to be treated is that if we did this there would be no pain, suffering, or sorrow. I saw that the sense of separateness causes us to hurt one another because we don't realize that when we only look to our self-interest, without considering the effect on others, we are actually exercising self-destructive behavior without consciously realizing it. It was shown to me that this was almost like an autoimmune disease where one part of the body doesn't realize that another part of the body is "self." This sense of separateness, I was shown, brought suffering into the world. In a sense it was the "original sin," bringing an autoimmune disease into the body of Christ (or God).

Dr. Raymond A. Moody, Jr., found in his research that several NDE subjects often reported a sense of connection with everything. He explains, "NDEers return with a sense that everything in the universe is connected. This is a difficult concept for them to define, but most have a newfound respect for nature and the world around them." He goes on to give an example. "An eloquent description of this feeling was given to me by a hard-driving, no-nonsense businessman who had an NDE during a cardiac arrest when he was sixty-two: 'The first thing I saw when I awoke in the hospital was a flower, and I cried, *Believe it or not, I had never seen a flower until I came back from death.* One big thing I learned when I died was that we are all part of one big, living universe. If we think we can hurt another person, or another living thing without hurting ourselves, we are sadly mistaken. I look at a forest or a flower or a bird now, and say, *That is me, part of me.* We are connected with all things and if we send love along those connections, then we are happy.' "[16]

On Society

- Truth transcends culture. Society perverts truth for social control.
- A society that asks "What's in it for me?" instead of "How can I contribute?" is a society that is doomed.
- If everyone knew their true nature, there would be peace on earth.
- Warfare is the antithesis of Universal love; therefore, there is no holy war other than the war within to lead a spiritual life.
- A few can deprive many of their liberty. It is up to the many to say "no" to the few.
- Individuals of a like group (such as races,

sexes, nationalities, etc.) are put into that particular aggregation in order to learn how to get beyond the particular interests of that assemblage.

- Just because "that's the way it's always been done" and "everybody does it," doesn't justify our action, or mean it's right.

- Each success in the world is our success. Every failure in the world is our failure.

- God created the plant kingdom and the animal kingdom to be interdependent; if one succeeds, the other succeeds. Conversely, if one is destroyed, then both are destroyed.

- Be in the world, not of the world.

- All are called to serve.

- The biggest obstacle to peace is too many special-interest groups.

- We are all believers of God. Some are consciously unaware of their subconscious belief.

- All creation is of God and is God's family.

Reflected Lesson
On Society

All creation is of God and is God's family.

During my youth I grew up believing that God is unfair. I was taught that when Jesus said, "I am the way, the truth and the life: no man cometh to the Father, but by me" this meant that only those who publicly profess their faith in Christ go to heaven. I felt if this were true, God is unjust because not everyone wants, or has the opportunity to be exposed to, Christian teachings. I asked the Light, which I call Christ, how people from other religions get to heaven. I was shown that the group, or organization, we profess alliance to is inconsequential. What is important is how we show our love for God by the way we treat each other. This is because when we pass to the spiritual realm we will all be met by Him, which substantiates the passage "no man cometh to the Father, but by me."

The Light showed me that what is important is that we love God and each other, and that it isn't what a person says, but the love in their being (we refer to this as heartfelt love) that is examined in the afterlife. In reviewing and reliving your life, your acts and thoughts of love bring you and God great joy, and your acts and thoughts of indifference, selfishness, and anger bring you and God deep remorse. We are all part of God's family, and are all interconnected. Those organizations, or religions, which claim some singular relationship with God, claim superiority over others, or exclude people for various reasons, go against God's law that we love one another as we love ourselves.

Dr. George Ritchie expressed his views on this subject in his book *My Life After Dying: Becoming Alive to Universal Love*. He explains, "We not only live in a universe, we are a universe. The greatest fault of man is that he has not understood this and he keeps making a 'diverse.' Religion has split us into a diverse, and so has medicine psychiatry with their worship of their own approach instead of seeing the whole."[17]

On Values

- Moral courage is recognizing your spiritual duty and doing it.
- Virtue finds friends.
- You should always honor your parents, even if you don't honor all their actions.
- Respect does not mean fear.
- It is best not to lower your values to accommodate others. Be the best example of the values you have.
- Kindness finds its way back to you.
- Our character is built by our dominating thoughts.
- The moral value to live by is to realize that

our rights entail responsibility. It is our responsibility to ensure that exercising these rights does not infringe on the rights of others. Good moral values require thoughts and actions which are beneficial to ourselves and others.

- We give glory through service.
- Feelings follow honor.
- Values are the criterion used to make decisions which affect the states of being and/or actions of self and others.
- Morals are the standards used in the thought process of discerning character, and exercising judgment in the actions of, and relationships with, self and others.
- The morality of the Light wants us to practice and follow thoughts and actions that help rather than hurt others.
- Happiness is the result of learning good moral values and practicing them.
- Honor is not synonymous with obey.

Reflected Lesson
On Values

Respect does not mean fear.

When I asked the Light about fairness, I was shown that many of the established religions of the world use fear to control their followers. This is based on their apprehension that they will lose power and money if their members seek another religion. I was shown that this causes a negative ripple effect. Many of the younger members believe their church showed no respect for other religions or other cultures, which leads to the growth of religious cults catering to the disillusioned. Without building on the basic foundation of respect, religions are destroying themselves from within.

The differences in world religions are predominantly cultural and we must learn to respect how others worship God. It is impossible to build moral values on a foundation of fear. The best foundation to build moral values is respect, honor, and love.

In his book *My Life After Dying: Becoming*

Alive to Universal Love, Dr. George Ritchie states, "I am charging the ones who have taught a religion of fear and hate, the ones who divide people into 'we' and 'they.' Catholics versus Protestants, Protestants versus Mormons, Christians versus Mormons, and prejudices in any form. Our world can be traveled in a day. My generation had trouble even accepting denominations that were different in the same religion. Our children are now in school, colleges, and universities with students who represent the religions of the world. The history of the human race teaches us that many wars have been started over differences in religious beliefs. We live with the knowledge that we now have weapons that can destroy the human race. We had better begin to realize that we all have separate realities. The merits of these realities had best be judged by which reality causes us to be the most kind, considerate and loving to ourselves and others." He later continues, "When I met the Risen Christ he wasn't impressed by what church I had joined, but asked me what I had done with my life to show Him. He was asking me if I had been kind and loving to those around me." Dr. Ritchie refers to those who used the Bible to justify preaching a message of fear and hate by interpreting the Bible as saying that those who do not agree with their interpretation are going straight to hell, as "modern pharisees."[18]

The Light gave us the same message: Love, not fear, is the foundation of the church universal. Respect and honor go hand in hand with Love. Respect does not mean fear. "Honor" is not synonymous with "obey."

On Wisdom

- Dreams are messages from your subconscious in the form of a puzzle. To comprehend your dream, piece the puzzle together.
- The wise person listens to their intuitive voice, then acts.
- The true aim of knowledge is to learn how to lead a spiritual life in accordance with God's will, not our will.
- The wise person has an inner sense of morality that keeps them balanced to prevent excess in any area of life.
- Using knowledge is far better than having knowledge.

- Wisdom is never irrelevant or irreverent.
- Seeking knowledge is a spiritual act.
- The beginning of wisdom is the knowledge that you don't consciously know everything.
- Grasping knowledge through reading helps us understand others who've lived before, somewhat like communion and time travel without leaving your chair.
- Knowledge is potential power, but knowledge with planned action is power.
- Every failure has in it a potential success.
- Power is structured knowledge.
- Focus on Love. Ignore hate.
- Focus on desire. Ignore jealousy.
- Focus on faith. Ignore superstition.
- Focus on hope. Ignore fear.
- Focus on enthusiasm. Ignore greed.
- Focus on romance. Ignore revenge.
- Change is constant.
- Truth brings freedom. Freedom brings happiness.
- Wisdom is the expression of infinite Love.
- Cheating is self-destructive behavior.
- Understanding is the key to wisdom.
- Knowledge is more valuable than gold. It is

something of value you can take with you to the spiritual world.

- Wisdom is the ability to use knowledge righteously.
- We can only gain what we are willing to accept.
- Pleasure is of the physical world. Happiness is of the spiritual world.
- Thought produces energy. Energy creates action. Action causes reaction. Loving thoughts produce love. Evil thoughts produce evil.

Reflected Lesson
On Wisdom

Knowledge is more valuable than gold. It is something of value you can take with you to the spiritual world.

I was shown in my life review that our purpose for being is to learn, a very powerful message. The importance of this message of learning was the reason I would have had to go back and relive my life again, from the very beginning. Suicide is like dropping out of a college course in the middle of the semester. If you want credit for the course, you must take it again from the beginning, and going on until completion.

Dr. Raymond A. Moody, Jr., reports in his book *The Light Beyond*, in explaining his research on the life review. "All of the people who go through this come away believing that the most important thing in their life is love. For most of them, the second most important thing in life is knowledge. As they see life scenes in which they are learning things, the Being points out that one of the things they can take with them at death is knowledge. The other is love." He continues, "NDEers also have newfound respect for knowledge. Some say that this was the result of reviewing their lives. The being of light told them that learning doesn't stop when you die; that knowledge is something you can take with you. Others describe an entire realm of the afterlife that is set aside for the passionate pursuit of knowledge."[19]

Afterword

I have known Sandi Rogers as both a friend and colleague for over two decades, and so have known her before her near death experience and after this experience. I have witnessed Sandi's numerous times of trial, and I have witnessed the truly remarkable transformation that accompanied her near death experience from a horrific suicide attempt.

Sandi's story is a fascinating case study of personality development and personal spiritual awakening.

Lessons From the Light are crystallizations of her own discoveries and eurekas as she went through the process of integrating her near death encounter with life as we know it.

I can attest, as both a longtime friend and impartial observer of her life, that her near death experience has had a profound effect upon her life and has influenced the lives of those around her as she continuously reaches out to be helpful to others in a committed and loving way.

Raymond A. Moody, Jr., MD., Ph.D.
Anniston, Alabama

Bibliography

[1] Eadie, Betty J., *Embraced By The Light*, Gold Leaf Press, Placerville, Ca., 1992, pages 104–105.

[2] Eadie, Betty J., *Embraced By The Light*, Gold Leaf Press, Placerville, Ca., 1992, pages 66–67.

[3] Eadie, Betty J., *Embraced By The Light*, Gold Leaf Press, Placerville, Ca., 1992, p. 51.

[4] Eadie, Betty J., *Embraced By The Light*, Gold Leaf Press, Placerville, Ca., 1992, p. 56.

[5] Moody, Dr. Raymond A., and Perry, Paul, *Reunions: Visionary Encounters With Departed Loved Ones*, Villard Books, New York, 1993, p.x [Introduction].

[6]Ritchie, Dr. George, with Sherrill, Elizabeth, *Return From Tomorrow*, Chosen Books, Waco, Texas, 1978, pages 56–57.

[7]Ritchie, Dr. George, *My Life After Dying: Becoming Alive to Universal Love*, Hampton Roads Publishing Co., Inc., Norfolk, Va., 1991, pages 23–25.

[8]Moody, Dr. Raymond A. with Perry, Paul, *The Light Beyond*, Bantam Books, New York, 1988, p. 11.

[9]Atwater, P.M.H., *Coming Back To Life: The After-Effects*, Dodd, Mead & Company, 1988; Ballantine Books, 1989, New York, p. 215.

[10]Ritchie, Dr. George, *My Life After Dying: Becoming Alive to Universal Love*, Hampton Roads Publishing Co., Inc., Norfolk, Va., 1991, pages 130–131.

[11]Ritchie, Dr. George, *My Life After Dying: Becoming Alive to Universal Love*, Hampton Roads Publishing Co., Inc., Norfolk, Va., 1991, pages 138–139.

[12]Atwater, P.M.H., *Coming Back To Life: The After-Effects*, Dodd, Mead & Company, 1988; Ballantine Books, 1989, New York, p. 132.

[13]Ritchie, Dr. George, *My Life After Dying: Becoming Alive to Universal Love,* Hampton Roads Publishing Co., Inc., Norfolk, Va., 1991, p. 136.

[14]Atwater, P.M.H., *Coming Back To Life: The After-Effects,* Dodd, Mead & Company, 1988; Ballantine Books, 1989, New York, p. 38.

[15]Kaufman, Doug, "Russian General Crashes Head-On Into Christianity," Belleville News-Democrat, Section C, page 1, October 1, 1994.

[16]Moody, Dr. Raymond A. with Perry, Paul, *The Light Beyond,* Bantam Books, New York, 1988, p. 34.

[17]Ritchie, Dr. George, *My Life After Dying: Becoming Alive to Universal Love,* Hampton Roads Publishing Co., Inc., Norfolk, Va., 1991, pages 57–58.

[18]Ritchie, Dr. George, *My Life After Dying: Becoming Alive to Universal Love,* Hampton Roads Publishing Co., Inc., Norfolk, Va., 1991, p. 112.

[19]Moody, Dr. Raymond A. with Perry, Paul, *The Light Beyond,* Bantam Books, New York, 1988, p. 35.